www.finishinglinepress.com

Rapid Redemption

poems by

Kay Reid

Finishing Line Press
Georgetown, Kentucky

Rapid Redemption

ACKNOWLEDGMENTS

Special thanks to Michael John Ward for his keen and thoughtful editing of
these poems.

Publisher: Leah Maines
Editor: Christen Kincaid
Cover: First Baptist Church, Ruleville, Mississippi, print. Kay Reid
Interior Photos: Kay Reid
Author Photo: Janis Khorsi, photographer
Cover Design: Leah Huete

Printed in the USA on acid-free paper.
Order online: www.finishinglinepress.com
also available on amazon.com

Author inquiries and mail orders:
Finishing Line Press
P. O. Box 1626
Georgetown, Kentucky 40324
U. S. A.

Table of Contents

These poems are for my son, Eli

And for the souls imagined in these pages.

Definition of re·demp·tion

ri'dempSHən/
noun

1.
the action of saving or being saved from sin, error, or evil.
"God's plans for the redemption of his world"
          a thing that saves someone from error or evil.

2.
the action of regaining or gaining possession of something in exchange for payment, or clearing a debt.

Preface

The characters in this book are imagined. Some indeed are based loosely and with exaggeration on real souls that walked the earth.

Gloria Dale

Darkness gathered in her pleats
a turquoise swell of summer skirt
Would she?
No, no, raise up a song to heaven
lift the right hand high
signal the soprano.

He, her husband
 watched
 admired
 adored
Up and comin' pair, GD and WL
Whitehaven Tennessee early fifties
hierarchies still prevailing.

Wrestling with the Lord proved good for them
He blessed their gametes
giving them twins
and a new ardor to follow
Him
in that way
in that way

Mississippi 2005
I their guest
delighted to tour
what they'd built and bought
churches
factories
barns
fields of tractors
fields of men

In the Hernando gates
Rhodesian Ridgebacks
silky in the sun
minded the estate

loving their people
though not all frangible creatures
sharing their acres

Inside
the sweet
Gloria Dale
recited
her novella about God's ways

Gloria Dale,
did I will myself to your door
to drink from your Rush?
All over the Pergola
his righteousness
videos, cassettes, Limbaugh till the end of time

But wait—
Gloria Dale
 you did know abyss
the deaths of daughters
the election of Barack Obama
cancer yourself
now a passenger on the final ship

GD your gleaming Lordspeech strange
even cruel
but goaded by love
you wanted daughter
 of Birdie and Erlis
not to be abandoned
to the devil's embrace

In this book, Gloria Dale,
 I return the favor to our lineage
and gather my characters.
          But please first tell me, what happened to the Dobermans
     who used to pastor the estate?

Rapid Redemption

      I. Golden Moon Casino, Pearl River Resort, Choctaw
At the bar for a bite
hanging in the smoke
we buzzed one another about our upcoming job
—the great chief, what would he be like?

Nearby, a bony elder with oxygen
chain-smoking Marlboros
napped on a couch in the lounge
between bouts of tables and slots

The poor, the blind, the lame
the robust and their offspring
lined up at the Rapid Redemption desk
to claim their wins
for some, surely salvation

Shawn, driver from Jackson the City with Soul
to the red hills of Neshoba, told how some faithful would
importune God
charging from church to the slots
Lord, if you'll help me
I'll give you half

The plump-lipped Chief
player and plain-spoken Moses
unromantic about his Indianness
or anybody else's
told us how he'd admired Germans
after the War
they built themselves up
he could do that for his people
Mississipppi Band of Choctaw Indians

      II. Amtrak, City of New Orleans
Cherishing the chief's Choctaw basket
I carried it on my lap

mulling the deliverance
he brought to thousands
in this poor state where I too was born

Across the aisle in coach, my neighbor's
minty scent and turquoise cross
broke the reverie
I prepared to meet my uncle
Memphis Central Station

Genial W.L., father's brother
drove us over the Hernando/Desoto Bridge
where family rumor says
Uncle's company was the builder
and he gave Blacks the high, dangerous jobs

   III. Hernando, Mississippi
Aunt and Uncle eager to embrace me
Swallowing liberal pieties, I loved it
Party thrown, everybody invited to ice cream
chubby twin and skinny one
the financier, the frail farmer
remembered when Gloria Dale would yay-ull at hee-um
Bee-ull, I could kee-ull you!
Just the kinda thing she would say
and not mean

The whole living room alive
those Choctaws, some of the biggest accounts
in Mississipppi
in updated hierarchies, the lowly Choctaws rank

   IV. Uncle's Study Upstairs
Pictures of Mid-South Fair
Uncle and Elvis, he and Gloria Dale with George and Laura,
Mid-South Fair and Mid-South Bible College, his beloved charities
Uncle the Inconsistent adored Elvis

told me how Elvis rented the fairgrounds
from sundown to sunup
so he and his friends could ride all night
He gave lots of money to Whitehaven churches
ah don't care about his wild parties and all
a good man.

Another wall, watercolor of Uncle's hunting lodge
on the Yazoo River
proud of the moat he built and the alligators
claiming the gators were to
keep out snakes
Ah want to take you there
Ah wanted to go
right then

Uncle made me sit for a minute
and listen to the story about a cousin
Sarah Louise and the coffins
her parents built in the middle of the night
down in Hattiesburg

V. The Hernando Kitchen
Old Bethel left for her own apartment
by the main house
Why, she's been with us 45 years and we jus see her as family

Over the island, Gloria Dale rendered her song
Ooh, Honey, we love you so much
we jus need to know
you know the Lord Jesus Christ
you are so sweet, but you know
there is a Hay-ull and it's HOT and it BURNS.

I kinda think of it in another light, I sputtered
you know the whole Body of Christ
neither male nor female, black nor brown nor white

kinda like a theology of nature, I said

Unsure of my fate
poor Gloria Dale
wrote me the name of a Bible preacher in Portland
she and W.L. had donated the land for his daddy's church
in DeSoto County
Now you call him when you go home
Gloria Dale drifted over to the kitchen window

It's kinda wantin' to rain, isn't it
Yep, it's kinda wantin' to rain.

Sarah Louise, according to Uncle

1.
Dad would come back to the Hattiesburg house with lovely pine; it smelled so nice!
  Cutting the boards according to dimensions
the family gave him, the coffins were a special shape, wider in the middle
  narrower at the top and bottom.
In the early days Dad hauled the lumber from town in our wagon.

2.
After Dad brought the finished coffin into the house, he'd return to the shop to
  make the outer box, which was put in the ground first. He'd come inside
then to help Mother,
who had already started lining the coffin
  with cotton batting half an inch thick or more. Over that she sewed in a
piece of muslin and finally, a thin silk, all from the dry goods store.

3.
For an adult, the coffin wouldn't be decorated too much
  but for a child it would be so beautiful inside. The prettiest to me would be
the pillow Mother made. The outside of the coffin was of a sculpted velvet fabric
  already designed for the purpose
Adult coffins were covered with gray velvet, and children's with white.

4.
I remember waking up early some mornings
  when my mother and father had just finished a coffin they'd stayed up all
night to make. Dad, who never, ever charged for making a coffin,
  delivered it to the family the morning it was finished.
My parents were especially kind, capable people, who knew how to do things to
help others.

5.
This was difficult for me as a little child.
It was a small community.
I was always aware who the coffins were for.

I knew the people.

Ruleville, Mississippi

From the oral history of Timothy, recorded in 2010.

Dad was chasing dreams
He felt his niche was cotton
Would put up a sign on a shack
E. A. Reid Cotton.

He like all the men in Ruleville
Tried to build himself a commission
between the seller and the buyer.

Mostly they just stood around
Shack after shack
All lined up, these shacks, all of them vying for the business.
This was The Depression.

I remember Dad walking home past a cornfield,
bringing home stolen corn for dinner
Then he planted some
And we had lots

It was in Ruleville where our father
bought a pig
Gutted and barbecued it in a shed out back.
All night long out there barbecuing this pig.
Roasting and turning it
Sold the meat the next day
Some people came by but he also
took sandwiches to town.

He was entrepreneurial, he was a dreamer.
Ruleville is where I have fond memories of falling in love,
With the carnival people.
The carnival set up right across the street Third Street
William and I went over and met these two girls, Pig Iron and
Scrap Iron.
I fell in love with Pig Iron and wanted to run away with her.

Pig Iron came home with us, and Mother, of course,
That child, has she ever had a bath?
I wanted to run away with the carnival
William did too
But he wasn't as enamored as I was.

They let us in the carnival free.
I cried when they left.

According to Mother

Daddy had prepared for her labor
filled the Plymouth
for the 10-mile drive from Ruleville
to Cleveland for my birth.

On the road through cotton fields
home to black sharecroppers
more destitute than Daddy
the car ran out of gas
Somebody probably needed it
Mother later justified, believed

Daddy walked to Ruleville for a can
returned to
his wife
 contorted
They would've just helped
I'll bet
if they'd come up and
found me in such trouble
Birdie's labor had stopped

When she finally delivered the baby
with forehead crunched wrinkled
and covering baby's eyes
The doctor warned
There's a chance she's gonna be blind

Rev. Ezekiel Jay Hill

1869 Neshoba County
youngest child of John Hill
who fought in the Civil War
and Elizabeth Tew Hill.

yielded to the call in 1898—
      how they said it when
        someone said yes to God
baptized more than 1,000 converts.
Pegged shoes, worked gardens and did anything to
help him get an education to preach the gospel
of the Lord he loved, his friend wrote.

Ezekiel, dead two years before my birth,
is upstairs on my second story
fleshy and beautiful in a portrait
 even important looking
in the way they painted them up then

The first and second of Ezekiel's wives died young
one in childbirth,
the other of "pneumonia of the colon"
Winnie, the third, the grandmother I knew
school principal
cleared their first Mississippi plot of Wild Onion, Wild Violet

used rickety hands to write reverently about her Ezekiel
as in this diary
He believed in staying with the dear old Book;
it must have the sanction of the Book before he will have it.

According to a story about Ezekiel spread by brother William,
a certain pastor in a Hattiesburg pulpit
preaching the moment that Ezekiel died
stopped in his pulpit on June 21, 1936
dead silent for a sec
declaring

Brother E.J. Hill has just died
in Memphis

That's 297 miles
to have your intuition cross.
Birdie Lee's tale of mortal Ezekiel more believable:
He could be severe
with us, and with cats
When he came home
and found a cat on a rocker
he made a terrible scene
Winnie Lee's cats were next to God
An entanglement to imagine:
cat talk with two stern
stubborn critters, Winnie and Ezekiel.

Winnie Lee

"Mudder,"
Birdie Lee's stepmother,
was from the Front Porch of the South
Louisville, Mississippi.

Mudder shook
and how she shook
lifting coal chunks into the stove,
inside the shed taking a hoe out
hoisting a bony finger
toward pupils who didn't dare not learn.

"Shaking palsy" it was called
but she who was afflicted to the eye
in a parallel life
an unruffled
unwavering Baptist
a quaking straight arrow
who could fell our father with a glance

No evangelizing, this Mudder,
not even father with his bourbons
nor the mamas and papas
of kids she reckoned with at school
Drop clues she did about the God
she turned her ears to .

Once, listening to the radio about Hitler
Mudder told me
she just *knew* she'd be with E.J.
in heaven after she died.
She knew it.

But it's how Winnie Lee went out in those
fields near Richmond, Kentucky
killing off copperheads and rat snakes
that incites me today—

She'd even scare off
a hungry snake circling the eggs
in a broody hen's nest.

Erlis' aversion to Winnie
less about her distracting tremor
than fear and trembling
before her strength
and constant eyes.

Erlis Audrey and the Afterlife

       Daddy
       poor cancered bones on the couch
       dying of lung cancer
       dying for a cigarette
       knew he'd sinned terrible
       tried to appease the Lord's wrath
       sent money to Jerry Falwell
       bought a large print Bible for the coffee table
       "preparing for his finals," said friend Catalina

       He feared the Lord real bad
       not as in *fear the Lord always*
       rather the place you're scared you'll go to after you die—
       Erlis, skinny holy unholy young cotton man who chose
       Ezekiel Jay's youngest daughter for his spouse:
       Mysterium tremendum

The Erlis Life
       four children
       worked like hell, got good at it
       drank, caroused, betrayed, told tales
       but provided, by God he did

After He Passed
       I asked kind Pastor Don Reid
       no kin of ours
       what Daddy'd confessed
       Sad Don said
       He could never do it,
       never tell me,
       never understand or
       forgive himself
       tried so hard,
       fought it clear till the end.

Young's Funeral Home
       Don declared

Like David, Mr. Erlis Reid struggled until his death
the remark pissing off a couple of pews

Unlike David
    Daddy is not in the Faith Hall of Fame,
    and I don't know that he didn't kill Uriah the Hittite—
    or what he did with those guns
    he stomped out the door with at 2 a.m.
His hate had me worried
    Snickering, *they want their rahts*
    also jealousies he had
    of other lovers of his women

    The gun period, then Father hit with a bout of gentleness,
    painted Kent State, sad about the carnage
    Old devil opened an art gallery
    wrote poems about birdies on fence posts
    made presents
    gave our mother a poodle
    me a little desk

Then his old self returned powerful

Erlis Audrey, my late years tell me
    had a magnificent shadow maybe monstrous
    he suffered lied died and was buried and we will not know
    what that ferocious energy could've saved, well maybe
    Central Africa, or himself.

Memphis and Whitehaven

Adults sang on screened porches
hummed into bassinettes,
plumped into swings,
clustered on church steps
heaping chicken on plates
at the picnic
.

Father (not in character)
cradled Wendell Willkie,
our little white terrier killed by a Ford.
Mother, in the house, chunked rhubarb into the crust
bore skillet corn
piquant and sweet to the bird mouths
in gravid air of Sunday 2 PM,
where at five the Crusade
would be launched at the bowl.

Slippery time down there,
preachers creaming up a salvation
where the sold trudge along
and the rich get away.

Yet *Tell Me the Old, Old Story*
I sang with the lot of them—
the God in that song so juicy, so kin.
Bittersweet
Memphis
and Whitehaven, Tennessee.

Revival and Red Taffeta

Wear your taffeta dress, it's Billy Graham!
My own Lady of the Book enjoined
It was mid-August, a Crusade at the Stadium
Reverend Graham the evangelist Mother saw as nearly God
        A lanky fellow whose team wore white suede shoes
        and refulgent ties to hug Harry Truman
        (who rebuked preacher's humid embrace)
        a troupe with spotless baritones

Yes mid-August, Memphis,
my ordeal was neither political social or even religious:
I was on a bleacher in the Memphis heat in a hot fabric
supposed to be a nice young lady for God

Sweat soaked through the seam and ruffle,
a ragged circle rendering red darker red.
Unable to stand for the "invitation hymn,"
Just As I Am Without One Plea
but that thy blood was shed for me. . .
Thankful not to be compelled
by white suede captains coaxing converts down the aisle

After the spectacle, joyous for some,
I begged Mother
as we slowly departed fairgrounds,
Walk real close
dangle your arm and purse around my waist
and cover the spot
She complied

I was thereby saved from at least one shame anyway.

Slumber Party

Whitehaven, Tennessee,
we were 13.
Suzanne, oh Suzanne
was there,
an elite Memphis apricot
and myself a mere entrail
in the local economy.

Suzanne, tanned from
noonday swims
in turquoise lakes,
was rumored to let boys
swim at her lips.

Suzanne, please
tell me what it's like when they do it,
kiss you on the mouth.

She didn't tell me but
how she showed me—oh Suzanne!

Papa Reid Had an Ethic

> that the old-fashioned could pull off
> Give tomatoes, green beans and suppers to the neighbor with tough luck
> Make the children work too hard and bring lemonade to the elderly
> Say *pleased to meet you* even if it wasn't true
> Talk frankly about rubbers to the young men and hired help

Papa Reid could have lived forever if
> only he hadn't worn his lean self out working the garden and business
> and taking care of Myrtle, disabled since her forties
> pulling her up out of the chair, taking her hands, gently pulling and
> guiding her
> walking backwards himself down the hall to the toilet
If only he hadn't made a u-turn near Elvis Presley Boulevard when he was eighty-
five.

Papa Reid fathered a multifarious garden
> One propagated his Success Roofing Company
> into an empire of concrete, cattle and oranges
> Others married or remarried pretty well
> sending out to the towns weird broods themselves,
> with the usual: cancers, religious conversions, disabilities, drinks
> and broody thoughts
And brood Papa Reid did that year when his turnips went wrong
and he had to rely on old Oscar to turn the bed around.

The Snooty Fox

Sharp and good lookin' Katie Jo,
1953 in Whitehaven,
borrowed black pumps, a sniffy suit,
head-hugging chapeau
for her bank appointments
to kick off a career in fashion shops.

Good soul, strong jaw,
ledger-wise,
Katie spun herself upward,
bettering not only her body's look
but joining her good husband's church,
Holy Communion Episcopal.

Retired when I visited her in Whitehaven, late 80s,
her husband deceased, she served chicken salad with celery bits:
I had been forgiven for trying to borrow money two decades earlier.
Stumbling to state our views in her airy dining room
 with flowers and pictures of flowers,

Katie became clear about one thing:
Some of them let their kids have bowel movements
raht on the floor in Safeway,
calling to mind what Uncle had said in the hearse
on the way to Mother's burial,
Y'all don't have enough of 'em up here.

Beverly Kay

Daughter of Jimmy Monroe, handsome drunk railroad man,
and Katie Jo, curator *Snooty Fox* shops, Memphis,
was born with CP and really good brains.
In Whitehaven, eighth grade, a shunning occurred:
I tried to walk from the bus stop not with the cripple
who bore my name
but with gorgeous
Charlotte, hoping her looks might rub off.

Savvy Beverly grew up to own motels,
Albert's Cabins, near Millington Naval Base,
her place famous among the locals.
At Albert's cousin hit pay dirt renting rooms often just for an hour,
some with garages for the guy who needed to hide his ride,
other rentals with ceiling mirrors, special sex channels.

Beverly also married well, he was smart & had CP.
The handsome, adapted home they built
featured in Memphis' *Commercial Appeal* full color.
Known locally for good deeds, Beverly Kay gave to veterans and
created a job for a mom whose daughter was murdered.

Out here in Oregon, one day, really broke
a single mother, I had called Katie Jo for a loan,
Beverly Kay's mom scolded,
Ahh can't believe you'd ask me that.
You know full well Beverly was born crippled and
just look how well she's done for herself.

Retired in Oregon, Daddy would use his special leer to
brag about niece Beverly's wealth,
her *ill got gains*, he'd grin the wide grin.

Known for her gambling, a person wrote in Beverly Kay's obit
she loved the casinos and playing the slots,
this revelation in the paper deplored by Uncle W.L.
He told me on the phone

Ahh just wish they hadna written that,
Hadna done that.
That was wrong.

Kentucky

Captain John Love

roomed next door in Richmond
at long unmarried Amy's home.
Amy, sweet on him, had to endure the fact:
John lives with his mother and her cat.

The warm and mysterious Captain Love,
a psychologist,
visited our home often,
too often, brothers would say
too rarely, thought Mother,
too queer, seethed Daddy
delicious, thought I.

In Richmond
and later the Jefferson Davis
John painted on my soul beautiful
Rhineland cities he'd walked before they were bombed out
Had a way of letting you know he felt bad about what happened
His gift of a music box
a Bavarian cottage,
serenaded me in my child blindness.
            Who in Lexington or Memphis had been to Bern and Vienna?
            At the Jefferson Davis, the melody would help mute mother's moaning.
The little skirt from the Philippines with rows of braided trim:
could John really give me such pretty things,
so many stories, so much praise,
and still be so terribly mean somewhere to someone?

Patti Sit

Was reincarnated into password
 in the twenty-first century
but on Lancaster Avenue early twentieth
she was companion Patti
imagined flesh and many words
on the porch with terrier Harriet and me.

Patti overheard the neighbor in a plaid dress
bolt to our porch crying loud
L.C.'s dead. . . L.C.'s dead. . .

 Patti knew it was 1943 in the world
I did not
she whispered the awful meaning to me and
ethicist Patti pushed other meanings too
scolded
when I on purpose dropped our
kitten from the top landing .

Patti's family then fell into terrible times
their house burned down
Mother and John Love
amazingly Daddy also
walked me around the block
to find the Sit home or its remains,
maybe we could help them I thought

but no the swirling blue came even had an odor
old leaves and cars
fell down the whole block
drenched the ashes of the Sit home
took out trees all of Lancaster
and Patti Sit disappeared

poof, poof gone
like L.C.
Patti Sit's lonely disciple now lost

made friends with the
woman in plaid
who missed her L.C.

The Jefferson Davis Inn
Lexington, Kentucky

My brothers Timothy and William,
     suited out in white coats
         bused tables at the elegant Inn.
John Love owned the Jefferson Davis
         and Mr. Love especially loved Timothy.

Our family's apartment upstairs, right by that of John
     and his mother, was paid for
         by young Timothy and William's labor.
            Our father, who had lost his job minding
               a munitions depot, loathed Mr. Love.

Upstairs, brothers also bused white pans to Mother's bedside
     while she wretched from radiation,
         her right breast still covered in white bandages.
            In time, Daddy landed a new job that put him on the
     road a lot.

Young Timothy ultimately became a wizard
     at turning John to dust
         Then the family got to move to Memphis for Daddy's work.
         Father's dislike of John did not abate with 423 miles
     between them.

I remain in the dark about dark John Love.
He was beautiful to the little girl I was.

The Jefferson Davis Inn later became a jazz club,
which still stands.

I want to find out what kind of jazz they feature.
Maybe go there.

Shrimpy at the Jefferson Davis

The ample orange cat had the run of the upstairs,
where very ample Mrs. Love, John's mother, cuddled and cradled her baby.
I hated that cat because it ate better than we did,
               Timothy told me, 70 years later.
We worked hard busing those tables after school and needed a snack.
We were hungry.   When nice old Earl
worked in the kitchen he'd sneak us snacks,
but a big broad Mrs. Love hired wouldn't let us have
even a tablespoon of ice cream.
Mrs. Love fed Shrimpy fresh, shelled rock shrimp—
she cooed him like an old fool.

None of us liked Mrs. Love, whose arm fat would jiggle
when she reached up for hat and coat.
I swore to God to never have arms like that,
but for Shrimpy, I guess they were pillows and all eternity.

Timothy, Betty, Mother and Daddy hated cats for decades.
William and I converted to cats when we were in our 20s.
about the same time we converted to Martin Buber,
from whom we probably both got the fact
that there is no conceptualization of a cat,
only an encounter.

The Dusty Boy

was on the street down a ways
from the Jefferson Davis Inn
where Davis himself walked
to Transylvania University

Dusty boy begged,
hung out near a little grocery
nearly naked.
Birdie Lee got wind of him
sent Timothy
with a shiny bar of soap and shiny apple.

The dusty boy hadn't been told
the Depression was over, the War nearly,
and that a sick-in-bed woman sent the gifts.

Kid sure didn't know about the stew the Inn was serving
or the young student at Transylvania 125 years earlier
a hero of the Lost Cause
whatever that was
who had walked the same street.

Captain Love at the Munitions Banquet

"I have never seen so much vice in all my life"
Righteous Mr. Love intoned
after cocktails and courses
at the Blue Grass Ordnance Depot
where Daddy was manager.

He is the most moral man I've ever met!
Virgin Birdie declared, and
adoration was not far from her
all the days hence

Erlis Audrey
Munitions Safety Director
hardly felt shunned

He had ordnance in spades.

Irving Pike, Neighbors across the Way

The farmer's daughters,
Mossie and Austin,
had different specialties.
Mossie was retarded,
Austin depressed.

Mother threw out the buckets of milk
Mossie brought to our porch; flies and God knows
what filth.
Mossie, staring at Mother, one day:
Mrs. Reid, I'm gonna kill me something,"
Mother, terrified:
Well, Mossie, what on earth are you planning to kill?
That fly on the swing, Mrs. Reid.
Mommy, she stops and stutters, I said.
Mossie's harmless, replied Mother, scared,

When their farm suffered a startling barn fire,
Daddy got the fire department out there right away.
Some animals died, but the house was spared.
The farmer thought Daddy was a hero.

Mossie just missed it all, and
Austin, poor Austin, didn't care
a few years later drank lye to kill herself.

Austin and Mossie's brothers both became lawyers.

Irving Pike, Our Mother

From room to room, Mother sang
My Old Kentucky Home
at the kitchen and at the coal stove
where she'd lift a flowered skirt
to warm the backs of her legs,
skin over the hamstrings red.

Her hands chapped and cracked from
washboards, sinks, hand-wrung mops,
Birdie sometimes got permed and primped,
but no salve for her hands
Balm in Gilead
she'd hum the one that makes
the wounded whole
otherworldly stuff in Birdie's mind
not cream for a woman's
Cloroxed hands

A fearless chicken assassin
Mother wrung the necks of birds
that became our Sunday dinner
but was terrified of snakes
in the henhouse.

Our old Kentucky home
was on a weedy, snake-ridden acreage
owned by the government,
the place we lived while Daddy
managed the Munitions Depot

A home not completely without warmth,
all of us sat near that stove
listening to the radio about Hitler, Jesus
and boys dying overseas

On Sunday we went on drives
maybe tried to get meanings from the preacher

Her birds went on making music all the day
as she traveled to new geographies
her Stephen Foster repertoire expanding westward
Beautiful Dreamer
she'd sing proudly proclaiming
to new Montana friends
I'm from the SOUTH.

Preacher Brother

Shining with oratory and a white Cadillac
William married an auburn-haired musical girl
and nailed big pastorates in his twenties in those
polite Kentucky churches with pillars,

Hundreds came to him for
consolation when JFK was shot
chairs out on the street
for the broadcast
from the pulpit,

Poor William, lovely throat,
though not a dabbler in callous religion
did step into shadow
going for the deacon's wife Rebecca
in need of consolation
in the post-op unit at Good Sam Hospital, Winchester.

Poor William, well of words and wordage
was in need of worship
Rebecca and William both had important wavy hair
and that helped.

William

Three Blondes at St. Vincent

You had to admire William, with
three nice ladies around the cranked-up bed:
one a gal he met in a bank,
one a budding novelist
      (younger than his youngest son—
      O Christ why say)
one physician's assistant:
The Adoration of the Blondes
at Saint William before The Surgery.

Each caressed his forearms, hands,
moles and faint hairs non-deterring
mildly drugged, William beamed
before yet another surgery
offering up the old near-death experience
he treasured
as an aphrodisiac
swilled by past admirers
not always blondes.

A question for St. Vincent and all the ages,
How did three healthy blondes share William's mere two hands?
Mysterium tremendum.

Lombard Pharmacy

Hunched on a walker,
Brother wears loose Levis,
his legs seep blood.
Crabby and demanding, he's here for pills.
Cirrhosis: medicine keeps him alive till his name
rises to the top of the list for a liver.

Lucky William got on the list
at the medical school
where he still snows teaching staff.
A counselor for sufferers of tinnitus
he regales patients and doctors.
The man of special gifts
declared to family in measured Kentucky bass:
    Ah'll get a liver because of my status up there.
Later, bleeding legs worse
wheel-chaired in the wait room,
he loudly announced (perhaps lied) to a cute aide,
    Ahh taught the Sound and the Fury at Ohio State
    Ahh taught a lot of Faulkner,
the volume of his flirtation
not concealing the shame working down
through sorrowed old viscera and seeping legs.

The Bill Hart Show

Dr. William Hart
lept, wept, slept
with the unconsoled and grieving,
the lonely and unraveling rich.
A few beneficiaries of his
advice and exquisite baritone
remained grateful to William
till his end.
Andrew, 90 now, is indebted to old Sundance
for riding with him through
the deaths of two sons
a drowning at the coast
and a crash on the way to the vigil there
the old father remembering,
yep, he always managed to get a smutty joke in, too!"

The Hart Show was devoured by an elder in the Valley
who funded William's horse-riding school
for disabled kids,
she felt betrayed fifteen years later,
that Mellifluous never stroked her mane.
Co-habitors never,
Co-coercers always.
His body. Her money.
But it's kinda even. Her kids tried to sue him
and didn't win, but they did put William out of business.
That business anyway.

Avamere Assisted Living

Here, William was adored by all sectors:
the enfeebled, the hale and the staff.
When able, he courted halls for new listeners.

Women and men would visit him, bearing blueberries,
caramel popcorn, computer gadgets,
movie classics, mostly Westerns.
Old Sundance returned the favors with flatteries,
verities, and good listening.

Peeing on himself from time to time,
made light of it
Ahh've gotta lay off that beer!

After Avamere, his neck dissolving from a surgery,
William was assigned to Vita Specialty Hospital
(for those sick unto the end).
Here immobilized in a halo vest
an appliance pinned to the skull
and clamped to the chest.

One aide, a ponytailed adorer
and a gymnast in her other life,
turned cartwheels for William at the
left foot of his bed,
just where he could see her,
and adore right back.

Dry Eyes

Moisturizing
eye drops
on a swivel table
not within his reach
his arm too weak to reach
aides installed them

Here withal
William argued with docs about God and time,
informed me importantly that
Dr Singh was more profound than
Dr. Blakely.

William and Helene

Only he could manage her genius
from the air grab
love letter scraps
story starts
legs of sonnets
written at Smith
50 years back
reassemble them with her.

William enjoyed the camaraderie
of her confusions
only he was mad enough
to steady her right hand as she folded
journal pages into hats or small Persians.

The oddity of her being
made him want to live
only William understood her religion
and her cat Shelley.

Helene to William

I've enjoyed a lot of things, thank God for that
I gave a carpet to the church
I gave part of a piano

Loving your children is something
I love the priest, the water priest
the French priest, too, back in school.

There'll be plenty of room for whatever
we have to say today
since there is no carpet in here.

The Old Bird

Did you save any of the Old Bird's
counseling shows?
the bright-eyed neighbor asked

She remains fond
had said no early on to his overtures and
 "that allowed me to love him"

Husband David, psychiatrist who
helped haul the nearly dead bird
off the couch on the island
black blood vomit
later eulogized the fibber and charmer
in a country song

That Terrible Night

on the way to the ER
with Dave, Timothy and me,
Old Bird asked brother to stop
so he could vomit
out the car door—
Managed to implore us
Please don't tell anyone about this
that I puked

Now in glory, nothingness
or pointillism
William needn't remember
the shame
that thing our father said to him
you got the ugliest feet I've ever seen

as William stood on the porch
in his wet dungarees
Keine wunder
 white Cadillac
lots of girls
and a little college presidency.

Birdie Lee

The World and Birdie at Her Menarche

> *1912, Rose Hill Fordham Lectures, physicians and analysts gathered,*
> *exploring nervous disorders. In 1913, eight thousand women took part in a*
> *suffrage parade in Washington D.C., with marching bands, banners and*
> *floats.*

And deep in another geography
Birdie Lee
was approaching her menarche
perhaps unaware of NY and DC.

The young lady with bangs
and good English
advanced to ever higher levels of
bookkeeping and Bible studies—

And with friends Sally and Omra
imagined futures sweet, husbands
though Ezekiel scolded his daughter
for talking to boys at church—
just when she was becoming luscious

Through young years of blood
the transcendental Birdie
pinned twice rinsed
cinnamon cloths to the line
little banners undulate
in the wind

Birdie would later allow
hugs if approved by God—
and then her Memphis evinced
she tipped
to a shiny guy
word suave
whose ornate promises
could curve a Lord thought into

three little iambs

Then the Depression
children
hard work for both
liquor he
nerves she
then 1980
my nerves are killing me

That she was loved by the above
through it all
Birdie Lee had no doubt

Birdie Thrilled

when Southern Baptists claimed Montana
Word spreaders quickly missioning
mines, buttes, Rockies,
scraping up souls

Brother Braswell
fresh from seminary
wore eloquent tortoise shell spectacles.
his pleas to the pews could dazzle
Dolce and Gabanna velvet collection
 comes to mind

Holding an impassioned fist to his lips,
brow wrinkled
he called people to forsake their
godless ways and come to Him
Old Pastor Goodnight, to his right, cried
when no new souls walked forward.

Mrs. Susan O'Dell on the left side of the nave
a brunette like Brother Braswell
 Hedy Lamarr lips
chocolate eyes
loved God and worried about hell so bad it awed me
she'd stare down her unsaved husband
elbow poking him during the invitational

I pondered—one in one out, saved and unsaved
were they able to be good neighbors?

Birdie's Burn Spots

Hot oil hit mother's
left wrist, printing
red spots on the thin
flesh over radial artery and vessels.
Boy, those places itch,
she told me in the Whitehaven kitchen
A hot Pyrex lid over
bubbling *Fritos enchiladas*
met Mother's hurrying hands
in Billings ten years later,
a red wedge rising out of right thumb.
Boy, those places hurt a lot.

Birdie kept on hurting herself,
surviving hot oils, coils, skillets,
until her tragicomic arms were too tired to lift.
Loathe for scars or burns to be seen,
she wore long-sleeved soft chambray
and gloves for Sunday services:
Enjoyed the sermon, Brother Braswell!

Birdie's husband, dramaturg,
proclaimed admiration for
his Christian in the kitchen,
but his sovereign of the oven
did not suit him in *la vie sexuelle*

And his ways she despised
her body surviving neither her duties
nor her spouse's spurnings.
nor minibars in the trunks of his Studebaker
and Olds,
certainly not his hurrying hands,
travels and chambers.

Women's Ward, St. Vincent Hospital
Mother's Pelvic Suspension Repair

Mother, returned from the green-slippered surgeon
and the abandon of anesthesia's vapors
crosses
from little death to speech.

Gold sheets and bedspread, gold room,
amending the whites of the 1920s.
Has the Caesar of linens
decreed a new color of death?

Floral caps on the aides.
Maids in pink.
Pearl-polished commode.
A pendulum of pipes.

Copper paper encases the mums
crisped for the hour of whimsy.
An incision colored in earth's
primal liquor.
Cinnamon-stained loins.
Over the sink, a crucifix.
The mouthwash is mint.
A catheter catches the aftermath of repair.
Four children hover with anxious breath.

Birdie Lee Crossing

My sick Baptist mother is near her end
her right arm a baked, popping yam
the rest of her dry and white as a tablecloth
back from the laundry for Sunday.

I can't open the fridge door with this thing anymore
that skin so shiny it could split
on bad days it hurts a lot.

She'll pick up a magazine that tells about
secret cures for cancer and open, frank
love affairs of gorgeous couples in L.A.

And that Southern Bible every day
She knows the skinny, rotten arm
and the good one will go to heaven together.

Rustling out back for a minute
tired from the sun, she comes in
I think I'll mash up chicken in the applesauce
scramble Rice Krispies with these eggs

I have a 2x2 photo of her when she was 20—
wide cute face, flapper bob, tuft of bangs
Stole it from the albums we play with.
Squirmy, picking fights these days
> *Did you bring all my pictures back?*
> *Of course*
Keep the one I lied about
on my top bookshelf
study it
as I soften for her death.

Muted

after a life with
exhausting Erlis
and fears that hugged
her pieces to pieces
the muted one advanced
to the final determination
after which exquisite Erlis
said of his late spouse
she was an outstanding grammarian

He meant I think
she didn't make
grammar mistakes
back when she spoke

Baylor University 1957
Guest Lecturer, Colbert Held

They are such beautiful people. . . It is unfortunate they are going to hell—

> *So you take pretty pictures of people you think God plans to roast?*

Scholar of spatial dynamics, diplomat
purveyor of one-way street
Dr. Held left the earth in 2016
perhaps in time he cast out the credo
then locked on his head

Sent Baylor way from "Little Korea"
Billings, Montana, where
cute guys at the mean high school
had shot up a farmer's house
to rape a slow girl
ohh why not rather a Golden Rule terrain

Baylor to be good learnin' and the Lord's people to boot
Birdie Lee joyful
Gloria Dale from Memphis
clapped and sang

Room 101 Ruth Collins Hall Baylor's new girls's dorm

      Roommate Gail
      so in love with boyfriend
      God the Baptist
      meant them to be together
      when on dates she smiled and told me
      they placed a rubber
      on the car dashboard and just stared at it

Handy window Room 101
      where bad girls crawled out
      met their guys
      back in at 3 a.m.
      entering my room from car hoods,
      a dangerous commute

You say anything about this and we'll cut your face up good.
You say anything about this and we'll cut your face up good.

Look again, Gloria Dale

I've the glistening Ridgebacks
looking a little hungry
 right by the chief and Birdie
near a row of Papa's tomatoes
and Erlis Audrey
in a sexy Studebaker

The red clay, coal
shacks on the mud and a ten bedroom
on Elvis Presley Boulevard
the dust on the dusty boy
 ice cream and its absence
at the Jefferson Davis
schools no end to
pupils of pinched teachers
we may have pinched back

I've John Love
long settled in a quandary of color
Timothy over the torture
William hunting blondes in the ether
eyes no longer itching

Assembled now.

Thanks for the fun work, GD.
Come take ice cream with me.

Kay Reid has spent the past 45 years chronicling communities and individuals in poetry, journals, articles. She has been the professional oral historian for several projects in the Pacific Northwest, including Portland State's Great Tribal Leaders of Modern Times, and Legacy of Hope, which documents social justice in the Catholic tradition. Today she teaches ESL and citizenship preparation to residents of her North Portland neighborhood. With 14 teens from Iraq, Burma, Somalia, she is also interviewing residents about their experiences of community, belonging and inclusion for the "Lived Citizenship" project. In the eighties, Kay spearheaded several efforts to help Oregon writers put their work into the world. During those years she also wrote poetry, spoke and performed it in venues ranging from tennis clubs to schools. After decades of documenting the stories of others, it is now her big job and her great passion to share more of her own written work with the world.

CPSIA information can be obtained
at www.ICGtesting.com
Printed in the USA
SHW011505210519
295FS

9 781635 349283